Journey

to

Myself

V.K. Robinson Enterprises

www.vkrobinson.com

(910) 723-2872

Scripture taken from the New King James Version®. Copyright © 1982 Thomas Nelson, Inc. Used by permission. All rights reserved. The Holy Bible, New International Version®, NIV® Copyright © 1973, 1978, 1984, 2011 by Biblica, Inc.® Used by permission. All rights reserved worldwide. Scripture quotations taken from the New American Standard Bible®, Copyright © 1960, 1962, 1963, 1968, 1971, 1972, 1973, 1975, 1977, 1995 by The Lockman Foundation. Used by permission. Scripture quotations marked (NLT) are taken from the Holy Bible, New Living Translation, copyright © 1996, 2004, 2007 by Tyndale House Foundation. Used by permission of Tyndale House Publishers, Inc., Carol Stream, Illinois 60188. All rights reserved. Scripture quotations are from the ESV® Bible (The Holy Bible, English Standard Version®), copyright © 2001 by Crossway, a publishing ministry of Good News Publishers. Used by permission. All rights reserved.

ISBN: 978-0-578-60432-9

Cover Creation by Vision Graphix
Cover Photo: Tasha Prescott Photography

Table of Contents

Dedications & Acknowledgements

To My Husband,

You are a man of few words and you like it simple. So just for you, I'll keep it brief. Thank you for over two decades of marriage. Thank you for putting up with me when I didn't like myself. Thank you for being willing to learn, what you didn't know in order to support me. I love you "Leroy."

To My Children,

There is NEVER a dull moment with you three. Much of my laughter comes from thinking of you all. When you all remind me of some of the things I did and how you all were brought up, I have to laugh. I love you all, three of you will always be one of the greatest joys in my life. I am thankful that God blessed me to birth such beautiful and kindhearted children. Thank you for enduring what you did not understand and loving on me during the hardest days. You all will always be my babies. I love you.

To My Champion and Greatest Cheerleader-

My mother, Annie P. Kelly,

We all have that someone that really needs no introduction and handles business at every juncture in life. That someone who really allows us to be who we are without judgement and without shame. Their love is limitless and their heart expands just to accommodate you and your shenanigans. That person for me is my mother, Annie P. Kelly. My mother has been a constant from day one June 16th 19... (wait you all did not really think I was going to give my birth year on this page, did you??). Throughout this process mom has been a pillar of strength and did not realize what was taking place. It wasn't necessarily her words that kept me-it was her will and her actions. Her actions said loud and clear, "Keep going, don't abort the process." Even in all that we have endured collectively as a family and as individuals, YOU my dear have been steadfast. Your faith has remained intact and your praise on ready at all times. Here I stand, Vanessa to some and Nessa to you, an author, and anointed scribe. I have grown, matured, and survived the tests of time and I was able to produce without an excuse. You have exhibited such tenacity, endurance, and strength throughout all of my life and I am proud to be your daughter. People tell me how much I act like daddy. Yes, I know I am silly, funny and quick witted just like him. But I get my will to survive and overcome from observing you and your steadfastness, intercession and faithfulness. My goal is always to make you proud and never make you cry tears of shame and regret-only tears of joy and gladness. Today is no different. Mom, this book, "Journey to Myself" The Reckonings of the Soul, is dedicated to you. I dedicate the birth of my first written baby to the awesome woman who was given the God honor of birthing, teaching, loving and chastising me. Here's to you sweet lady. There is only one Annie P, and I am so glad God trusted the gentleness of your hands with the tenderness of my heart. I love you, Gal!!!

To My Siblings,
Tina, Arlene, John, Renee, Matthew and
Valisha

Life for us hasn't been a bed of roses, but we are still here. I am thankful to each of you for just being you. I sit as the middle child among some pretty awesome people. You all have proved the doubters wrong and you are still standing strong. In your own way, you have taught me resilience and how to fight. How to go after what I want no matter what. Each of us holds pieces to our father. All of us have some of his wittiness about ourselves that is sometimes scary. Thank you for loving me and being on my team. I couldn't choose you but just so you know, you are stuck with me. I say to each of you, keep being great. I love you.

To My God Mother,

Betty Buie McLain King, the woman for whom I am named after. You who showed me tough love and nurtured me at the same time. I was able to call you when I really thought I was going to die and you held me up. While you are not physically here with me, I hope that I have made you proud. You were there from the beginning until God called you home and I will always appreciate and remember who you were and what you stood for. I haven't forgotten the heart to heart talks. They push me on the hard days and remind me that although quitting is always an option for someone, it is never an option for me. Thank you, Ma Betty for just being you. The journey has been far from easy, but I am still pressing forward. Terri, Betty, James & Ophelia, and Roger, thank you for sharing Mom with for all those years. I am honored to have such awesome older siblings to look up to even now.

To Ophelia,

Sometime ago, I received a text message during the day from one of my dearest sisters. She sent me a text to ask if I could talk. Now, initially I thought something was wrong because, 1. She never sends text messages during the day and 2. She told me to call her at work. Those two NEVER HAPPEN unless it is an emergency. Well, I am glad that she was driven to converse that particular day. During that random conversation, she and I shared such beautiful things in reference to our relationship with God, prayer, and journaling. I laugh because not one conversation ends without us talking about books. As a matter of fact, we were both online looking up and ordering books. *Thanks goodness for gift cards and prime.* Following our conversation, she sent me a photo of her journal collection.

Now these journals were not all purchased. They were not all perfectly bound, printed and fancy. Some were created and tacked together. Some had been clipped together because of extensive use. Nevertheless, their purpose was served. Sometimes it may have been to release a pressing matter, other times to record of a process, to scribe dreams and interpretations, to write down strategic prayers, to jot down gains and losses, and to be kept for the purpose of jarring memories once the mind begins to fade. Whatever the purpose for the journals, it was intentional and well thought out.

Ophelia, your lessons have spanned from my teenage years until now. Every conversation we have there is something that I gather from your field of plenty.
You, my darling, are a precious jewel and a blessing. Anyone in your presence can glean from your fruitful trees and become better with the application of the lessons. You have such a passion for prayer and the people of God that pours over into the lives of all those connected to you. Thank you for embracing me, teaching me and loving me through some of the toughest times in my life.

The journaling component of this release is dedicated to you, Ophelia M. McLain. I love you and I will always remember the importance of journaling because of you.

Foreword
By Dr. Ophelia M. McLain

I met Vanessa over 30 years ago through my then boyfriend. Our connection was immediate. We shared hearts and secrets. I had the privilege of being her eldest child's godmother and had the pleasure of her serving as my bridesmaid. Over the years, I have seen her mature from a caterpillar which thought this was the life, through her cocoon stage of the many challenges that brought her to this beautiful, colorful butterfly stage. Her resilience has been made possible by many, most notably, my mom, Betty Buie McLain King. She took Vanessa under her wing and was very clear on her place in Vanessa's life and her role as a mentor and a shoulder to cry on. Vanessa took every opportunity to glean from her spiritually and through life application. One of the things that I have noticed about Vanessa is how grounded she is. While she can eloquently share spiritual truths afforded to us through the Word of God and can powerfully war in the spirit for others, she is relatable to the everyday struggles people experience. In this book, I have no doubt that her experiences will help others see that they too can survive, and that she will share tools to help others breakthrough the many barriers they face.

The Introduction

For years I struggled with who I was and who I was not. As a result of that struggle, I walked daily as a casualty of my own war. Although I was screaming on the inside-I understood- we don't talk about things like "this" in public. We don't uncover ourselves. You wipe your tears, you dress up and you do what you're supposed to do. I was unable to be transparent about that part of my life because I feared that others may have judged, shunned or labeled me as the local crazy. Nope, I dared not to share. In my fairy tale vision, that chunk of my journey was nonexistent. For years, I treated it as a blur although it was very vivid in my mind. The debate to convince others to understand the rawness of the battle wasn't worth the hassle. My quick fix was church. I ran to the church. I hid in the church.

I hid behind a shout and a dance. I hid behind singing and seeing others set free as I ministered praise and worship. Even though I ministered from a broken place, I received a silent, "atta-girl" for just pushing through. I am not discrediting or mocking the church. I am simply sharing where I was in my life.

On more than one occasion, the church- The

Body of Christ, saved my life. I grew up in church. Being active in ministry was my saving grace. Church was my safe place. I knew once I got to the church that all would be right with the world. Honestly, it was a given for me. That is what I knew, "Just get to the House of the Lord." I did – I got to the House of the Lord. I did all the right things, at the right time, in tune, on key, in step and in sync with what was expected. Even though this was my routine each time I went to worship- I always avoided dealing with the inevitable. I couldn't seem to touch the aging battle that was raging on the inside. The best solution for what I was feeling was to get around fellow believers and partake of what should've been a life changing word in my life. Yet, my truth was that no matter how much I'd danced, sang, clapped, wept, shouted and ran around the church, sat and listened to the Word, when it was all over I still had to go home. There was indeed something blocking me from going forward with the application of the preached word.

At home. I was still a wife and a mother but the torment I experienced was gut wrenching. It wasn't fair. I tried but I could not articulate what I was feeling, how I was feeling or why I was feeling that way. The burden of shame gripped me and yet I continued to simply exist. I existed to do what was expected of me. I couldn't let my husband and children down. I couldn't let ministry go unfinished. I couldn't tell anyone what I was really feeling because it was just that- a feeling. A feeling that would go away, Right? Wrong….

I was joined to the ranks of many who had the faith that would heal cancer, regulate high-blood pressure, diabetes, to bring anything that is out of line into alignment and all of the other illnesses you can "touch." But what about the illness that can't be touched and identified with blood work, CT scans, MRI's or x-rays. What about depression and anxiety-the illnesses that are often brushed off as just spirits. There I was in the church, "going on with God anyhow" and fighting just to function from day to day. Yes, I just wanted to make it. I did not know what to do or how to do it. It was almost as if I was stuck in a time machine. I couldn't move forward and I could not move backwards. Every time something traumatic happened in my life I was sealed tighter into the time warp.

The truth is that there is an astronomical number of people in the church, battling in their emotions and are simply functioning to survive one moment at a time. Many people suffering, living with and enduring untouchable, ignored and overlooked illnesses are just like I was, stuck. I remember hearing a preacher say, "No Christian should ever suffer from what the world calls 'depression'. We should believe God for deliverance from that spirit, get up out of that pit, rebuke the devil and give God praise." I am fully aware that this statement was not ill- intentioned. Yet and still it was a slap in the face to those who suffer from depression and other emotional situations that they do not have a handle on. This statement is one that is not always spoken but understood. It is understood to the point that each time it is spoken or implied, instead of giving hope, it adds a layer of isolation to those wanting to be free.

As Christians we preach, teach and expound on prosperity, deliverance, supernatural breakthrough and so many other great faith-based manifestations. Yet, one of the things we don't specifically address and include in the aforementioned categories are those emotional challenges. Sometimes we make it our business to keep these on the invisible, "DO NOT TALK ABOUT LIST" and leave them isolated on a shelf with the hopes that it will just pass. The church should be a safe place, right? Remember, we would always say, "Come as you are." However, sad to say church is the one place where emotional challenges such as depression are often viewed as the pink elephants in the room. Some don't believe these are real illnesses and characterize them as a spirit or someone is just acting out. Some have the misconception that unless you are wandering aimlessly, homeless, unemployed and overmedicated, that you are not suffering from anything other than a spirit. It is then slid under the rug with hopes that it will disappear with time.

I too once believed it was a spirit and in my mind, I could praise my way out of what I was dealing with. Today, I uncover myself and admit that was me and my perspective- I could not have been more wrong. As a matter of fact, it wasn't until I had to deal with myself, my inner struggles that I realized how blind and wrong I had been for so many years. The truth of the matter, I was struggling in my faith and tormented in my emotions. I was fighting whether to seek professional help and take medication for whatever I had going on. My detour was my hiding behind the facade of doing church and having church while I was dying inside and a prisoner of depression and many other unanswered sufferings. Yes, you read it correctly, depression. I was crumbling under the weight of depression. My dancing, shouting and singing were only bandages covering the cracks, creases and open wounds of my broken spirit.

I am taking the time to be transparent. I know some people may not need the book and may just cast it to the side. However, for those that can relate, need healing, need to know that someone has been where you are and you can be free- today is your day. I encourage you, take a deep breath- inhale-exhale- just breathe. Take my hand as I share my testimony. You are not alone, you've got this!! You are going to make it! Let's Go!

Just in Case You're Wondering...

My husband has been a professional truck driver for over twenty years. Therefore, when we travel he does all the driver. I dare not complain because distance driving is not at all my forte. When he is driving I am usually, reading, writing or sleeping. I don't really pay attention because I trust him to get me where we are going. He never disappoints. One day while driving to visit family in another state- I actually paid attention to the highway. I noticed the green road signs with numbers sitting over to the side of the highway. I asked my husband what they were and what they meant. He said they are mile markers. Things happen on the highways while traveling from destination A and destination B. Often times incidents occur while the travelers are in between major exits. Car accidents, medical emergencies, mechanical issues, or someone being lost all happen on the highway. Since emergencies are not tied to major exits, the mile markers, allow the person calling for help to give a general location to get the assistance they need. Once he explained, I was glad I came to understand the rhyme and reason of it all. Since then, I have been more attentive to the mile markers when driving.

While making notes for this book, I looked at life

as a journey and the fact that we are always between point A and point B. The obstacles we encounter do not appear at convenient moments. On the contrary. Most of the time when life "happens," it is usually at the most cumbersome times in our lives. Those happenstances compound drama, trauma and stress that we are already battling. We often say, "Lord if one more thing happens- Lord, I just can't take another thing."

To further complicate things, we tend to compare our journey with that of other people. In doing so, we become confused, frustrated, angry, and withdrawn. Our focus is no longer on our journey. Our eyes are zeroed in on everyone else. Thus, causing us to lose valuable time that we should dedicate to our personal journeys.

Our journeys are uniquely designed and present us with a mirror of who we are at every juncture in our lives. One of the downfalls of the mirror is that we often don't want to acknowledge what we see. Like myself, I went years living as who I wanted people to see. I lived the life that I thought people accepted. I lost time, I lost connections, I lost opportunities and so much more. Once I accepted the journey and everything that came with it, the good, bad, ugly, painful, confusing and all other life happenings-I learned that all the things I'd endured, was enduring and would endure serve as mile markers as I travel the highway on the "Journey to Myself."

I've come to know that the soul is immortal, inner part of my being. When one mentions the soul, it is usually in reference to inspiration, joy, refilling, and awakening. However, sometimes the soul is the house for sadness, torment, rejections, abandonment, confusion and other negative, but very real residue from the not so pleasant occurrences in our lives.

A reckoning is where one takes the time to come to a place of resolve. Resolving, settling all of the aforementioned lingering residue within ourselves. Our souls can house layers upon layers of residue from unfavorable experiences. Those layers tend to serve as blockades, preventing us from experiencing true personal freedom.

I decided I wanted to be free. And in order to be free I had to deal with me. To deal with the troubled state of my soul and hidden parts that I had masked for years. The process of peeling through and removing these layers was difficult. Yet, I opened myself to dealing with my buried truth so that I could be free. Hence the subtopic, "Reckonings of the Soul."

When you travel long distances, there are rest stops along the way. Sometimes you have to stop and stretch your legs, rest your eyes, take a bathroom break, get a snack, revisit the map, check how far you've driven or how much further you have to travel. It is a perfectly normal part of a trip. As you read, the ending of each chapter has a rest stop. These stops will give you time to reflect and journal in response to the content, the questions asked, the questions that come to mind, or just your thoughts and personal position as it relates to the content. It is my hope and desire that you just not read through the book so you can see the things I've endured. I want you to interact with the content. Most importantly, as you are reading and responding, I want you to know that you are not alone.

Mile Marker 1

Dance of Denial

*The heart is deceitful above all things, and desperately sick; who can understand it? "I the L*ORD *search the heart and test the mind, to give every man according to his ways, according to the fruit of his deeds." Jeremiah 17:9-10 KJV*

Dancing is an act where partners join together for a performance. No matter what method of dance one uses, the dancers are always in motion and moving from place to place. The dance of denial tends to have its participants moving away from the very thing that needs to be confronted. For me it was the fact that I had some things I needed to face that had been buried for years. The deeper the grave the more painful the exhumation. The dance of denial is either at an upbeat or somber pace. In dancing partners choreograph a routine and practice intently in order to perform it to crisp perfection. Both partners can be excellent dancers but only one of them can lead. In this particular dance, Denial takes the lead. Denial busies you and draws you away from the reality of your situation. I had become intertwined with denial. Flawless to a fault but perfecting for the final performance. And if for nothing else- it is because your reputation is on the line. I looked good, spoke well, and performed well, but the harsh reality was that I was broken and it was only a matter of time before the performance was over and I would face a not so favorable end.

My vulnerability caused me to be handcuffed by the bond of denial and pride entangled me in the wilderness of depression. The two of them together were at the top of their game and I was nowhere near ready to compete with these two beasts of oppression.

As a child, we have a vision of what we want to be and how we want to look. Then WE plan how we want the world to view us. Based on that plan, we learn how to dress it up. In the natural, dressing up is fine. When it comes to dressing up matters of the heart, we end up in a tango with denial. We, don't want to accept the entirety of who we are. For me, that was depression. Is that you? Have you dressed up and covered so many years that you really haven't embraced the entirety of who you are? Have you been hiding your torment to the point where you have learned to live with it? Have you said, "that's just the way I am?" I have to challenge that thought process and tell you that, NO- that is not just the way you are. On the contrary, there is indeed a root.

Looking at me, you could not tell I was depressed. You could not see that I was on the edge of a nervous breakdown on multiple occasions. Why? Because I wore the mask and denial was in charge. You could not have told me I was depressed. Why? Because if you told me that, I would have blatantly denied it. That was when my Tango began. Like some of you, that kind of living became such a part of me- that I had accepted it as just that, my life. I would talk to and convince myself there was nothing wrong me with me. Life just hit me sort of hard, but I am going to be just fine.

Dressing up the outside was for validation and approval. I was able to check that off as mission accomplished. The outer layer looked good and the compliments whether articulated verbally, through a smile or a head nod were numerous. Yet, there I was, a fragile shell of a woman looking jazzy and altogether on the outside and slowly cracking from the inside out. As long as I looked good, I convinced myself I felt good. And if I felt good, I was good. While it can hold true in some cases, for the peeling of this layer it was not. I was in denial. Camouflaged within the term denial is the term "l-i-e." I had to lied to myself for so many years that I had to figure out the truth. This truth was that I was in a dark, dry, desert place. Yes, the wife, mother, minister, praise and worship leader, encourager, professional, bubbly, happy go lucky, life of the party, sister, friend, daughter was in a dark, dry, desert place. I was so fixed on being who I thought people wanted me to be that I didn't take the time to deal with my truth. I was saving the world, helping others, succeeding in the workplace, solving other people's problems and watching them earn wins. I was so caught up with looking good and tackling stuff that by the conclusion of each day I was so tired I couldn't deal with my own troubled heart.

On the inside, I was wailing. I was broken and desolate.

The routine continued for years. It's as if I was so dressed up and put together that I could never get the release I needed because it would've tarnished my image. I couldn't release how I really felt. In my mind, depression carried a negative stigma and I wouldn't *allow* myself to be in that situation. I told myself daily, "No Ma'am you will not break down. You will not let them see you cry." Especially since I had no idea why I wanted to explode in tears most days. I just knew, I was dressed up and the tears I wanted to cry had no purpose. Therefore, I wouldn't allow myself to release. Tears and screams sat in my throat many days, but I washed them right back down and kept stepping to the beat of my own drum.

I am a happy, energetic, and lively person. The person that will find something to laugh about and make those around me laugh as well. Even while sad, depressed and fighting anxiety- I held true to who I was. When I go on doctors' visits, I smile, speak to everyone, and often times hug. This particular day, I did nothing out of the ordinary and patiently waited to see my doctor. I wasn't experiencing many external symptoms. I just knew I wasn't feeling "right." I got into the patient room and sat on the exam table. As the nurse took my vitals, I encouraged and told her how beautiful she was. My blood pressure was elevated some. This was a follow- up appointment from blood pressure irregularities, so I knew the doctor would address it. He walked into the room, put his hand on my shoulder and greeted me as he always does. Within moments, the floodgates had opened. The dam had been breached and the tears would not stop. I cried like a baby for several moments. He did not interrupt. He did not rush me. He just sat there and allowed me the time cry it out. Once I was calmed down, we talked about my vitals. Because of my blood pressure, he recommended I take some time off from my job. I cried again, time off of my job was the last thing I needed. My job gave me validation. My job gave me an escape. My job kept me busy.

He continued the conversation by recommending that I seek therapy for depression. I quickly straightened up and said with a matter of fact tone, "Dr. A this isn't depression, it's just a bad day." I thanked him for my safe place and moment of freedom and left. When I crossed the thresh hold of that door I looked just as happy as I did when I walked in. I said my goodbyes and exited. There I was sitting in my car, thinking, "He's usually right but this time he is wrong. I am not depressed." I drove and filled my prescriptions and life continued. My dressed up broken self - had assumed my abnormal normal. I did not share the information with anyone. In my mind, it was something else, an additional scar or bruise that I would have to work hard to dress up, but the truth was, it had always been there. I did not know what it was, so I did not acknowledge it. Now, I knew what it was and the negative connotation of depression made me want to suppress it more. Within three weeks I was back in the doctor's office and it was almost a deja-vu moment. My blood pressure was better but not where it needed to be and I was a hot mess emotionally (behind closed doors). He gave the same advice and recommendation. This time he took me out of work for a few more weeks. It was after this visit, I halfway listened. While I was on medical leave. I begin to research counselors and therapists. I was cemented in denial and I opted to go to a counselor just to prove nothing was wrong- I was not depressed. If I was going to do it, it had to be my way. I had a few non-negotiables to support my search. Let me just say, they seem quite silly now.

Initially, I did not take the time to share the details of my "issue" with anyone-not even my husband. I kept him in the dark. I did not want to explain what was said about me. How could I share or explain it- especially when I did not believe it myself? By doing so, I would have been forced to accept something that I was not ready to accept. Again, denial had taken the lead and I was still in a mess.

(Disclaimer: I would not recommend any spouse
  handle things the way I did. By doing so I created an environment that worked against me for some time.)

I arrived at an office in what seemed like a top-secret location. It was off the road and the outside of the building did not scream, "this is a therapist's office." I walked in looking over my shoulder as if I was making sure no one saw me. The office was subtle and calming- but I was very uncomfortable in the waiting area. I remember looking at the ceiling fan to avoid having to look at the numerous pamphlets about depression and anxiety. I did not want to see the plethora of help phone numbers to call. I looked towards the television and it was an ongoing infomercial about getting the help you need. Beside the television was a sign that said, "DO NOT TURN THE CHANNEL." Well, there went that idea, so I sat and stared at the ceiling fan. Planning what I was going to share, what I wasn't going to share and how this was going to play out.

Let me interject here that while this part of my life was spiraling, I was still going to church and active in ministry. I did not dare breathe a word of my woes to my church family. It was a spirit remember? You pray it off, you leave it at the altar and then you give God a dance of praise. Nope, that is not how this would work it out. Please don't misunderstand. I am a praise and a worshipper and I love giving God my best praise.

But in this case, my situation-praise needed to be partnered with some external resources more than I knew. I wasn't praying about it and leaving it with God. I should've been but I was not. I kept my hand in the way. It was like playing a poker game, I was only showing what I wanted seen. I was only revealing the needs I wanted to be met. I would lay my emotions at the foot of Jesus and when the crying stopped, I gathered it all and returned to my abnormal normal. Have you ever claimed to give it all to God and trust His plan-only to continue dabbling in it your way? If you answered yes, don't worry-you are not the only one.

A beautiful woman calls me into her office and we chatted. Oh!! Yes baby!! I knew exactly how this "session" was going to go down. Or so I thought. I thought I would go in there with her, share the information from my doctor, tell her how strong my faith was, exchange religious jargon, have a praise break, and make my exit. It sounds funny now but I really thought I would be able to control what was getting ready to take place. Boy, was I ever wrong.

We spoke of things that I vowed never to release into the atmosphere. She took the time to explain what depression was and the fact that it affects people in different ways. The initial conversation was only a basic exchange. As our visits continued- the powerful yet subtle way, she allowed God to use her to maneuver through my menagerie of hidden hopelessness was intriguing. She poured alcohol on my lie and moved it out of the way as she stoutly but gently removed the tattered bandage off of my reality. With that firm motherly tone and a look that said, "you know I am not about to play with you," she forced me to face some things head on.

It was on that day that I was introduced to depression. Tears, shaking, and fear of the unknown. I was able to put a name to the part of me that I fought not to accept or acknowledge. Little that I know- this was just the beginning of the journey. That day, I looked in the mirror and said to said, "Hello, my name is Vanessa, I am a Christian and I'm suffering from depression."

Now before I could even inch towards healing I had to be honest. You must take the time to be honest with yourself about where you are. My nice clothes and high heels on the outside could not erase what I was dealing with. I needed help outside of the church. Scriptures were good, worship was good, preaching was good but this was so much deeper than routine worship. I just did not want to admit that mine was that deep. Uh huh, yeah, I had to deal with the REAL ME. I did not understand how troubled my heart was. I did not understand that I could not pin point the root. I thought I was going to feel better. No, on the contrary, much to my dismay, when I accepted the diagnosis things began to fall apart and I had no control.

On my hard days, when things seemed to fall apart, I was truly grateful for my oldest daughter. When I was too broken to parent- (I call those my "parenting on pause" days) she would do her sisters hair as best she could, prepare food and anything else I needed her to do. She didn't fully understand but she knew mommy needed her help and did her best to make it better. Her sincerity made the days easier to maneuver. Yet, deep down inside I was beating myself up because I could not be the mommy I needed to be. I was letting my children down. I was a disappointment to them. Or at least that's what I thought. As badly as I wanted to, I couldn't find the words to explain to them what was going on with me. I was the one that was supposed to hold them together. I was the one that was supposed to be their rock, yet there I was in our home with depression chiseling me down to mere crumbs without an explanation.

I'd heard and used the cliché, "things are going to get worse before they get better," but it did not ring true until this point. I continued my sessions until things balanced out. It became easier. Yet, something else happened I went down again. Only now, I knew why I was going down. I knew "it" had a name. I was no longer in denial and my dance marathon with denial had ended.

Rest Stop 1.5

Take the time to pinpoint when you realized you were really suffering from depression or another emotional challenge. Did you accept this initially? Did you share it with anyone? How did you cope with this realization? Use these guiding questions to journal your thoughts and how you entered your process. You may have to put the book down and walk away and that is perfectly fine. Take a moment and regroup. Inhale- Exhale- Now write without fear of judgement or being discarded. Write with one thing and one thing only in mind, YOUR FREEDOM.

Personal Declaration and Affirmation

Let me first congratulate you for choosing to take the first step. I know you have been suffocating emotionally for some time but today you have taken a leap of faith. You have given yourself permission to breathe. To release the truth that has been lodged in the pit of your belly like a cinder block with no wiggle room. So again, congratulations!! I celebrate your first steps today.

Repeat after me: Today I vow to be honest with myself and transparent on these pages. I no longer have to be ashamed of my depression. I am not a reject because I deal with depression. I am not an outcast because I deal with depression. I am fearfully and wonderfully made. I am a beautiful creation. I will not allow this moment to pass by. I will be an active participant in my journey to freedom. Even if that means I need to get professional counseling or join a support group, I will stay the course to my Freedom.

Prayer

Dear Lord, I come to you on behalf of the one reading this prayer. I thank you for their life. I thank you for their willingness to take the journey towards the better you have in store for them. Lord, I ask right now that you would give them the strength to keep pressing through. We cast down shame and fear of transparency. For we know that it is only through being totally honest with ourselves that we can remain on our journey to healing. I pray against the negative thoughts that may come to through the enemy, the inner me. The thoughts that will try to sway us that we can never be whole. The thoughts that scream we will be stuck in this rut for the rest of our lives. I cast them down now. I declare that healing and wholeness is their portion. In your name we pray, Amen

Mile Marker 2

Exhausted: Too Tired to Quit Too Tired to Keep Going

"Come to me, all you who are weary and burdened, and I will give you rest. Take my yoke upon you and learn from me, for I am gentle and humble in heart, and you will find rest for your souls." Matthew 11: 28-29

Exhaustion is a state of being overly tired. I was at a point of exhaustion that I was too tired to quit and too tired to keep going. My mind was running like a runaway freight train and I did not know how to stop it. I could not seem to catch up with whatever was going on in my heart and mind let alone what was happening in my life. Exhaustion for me was a huge clump of matted residue from my depression.

Let me explain, while I was working hard to continue putting forth my best effort and focus on healing-life was still happening. Every hit reminded me of how tired I was. I was mentally tired and physically tired. Even my tired was tired. My days and nights ran together. A decent night's sleep was a memory of the past. I stayed in place. I kept going to work. I kept going to church. I kept fulfilling ministry obligations. I smiled through it all. I saved face and never used the word "no." Yes, I was exhausted. But there was a part of me that needed to be needed. Being needed helped me not have to deal with how tired I really was, and how to get untired.

During the time of my major exhaustion I was pregnant. I had to have a surgical procedure called a cerclage, to keep from going into to pre-term labor. In addition to the surgery, I was placed on complete bedrest. My son had quite a few inner ears issues and my husband was on the road. This meant that I was the one taking my son back and forth to the otolaryngologist. Because of being on bedrest my husband and I decided to take my son to Alabama with his parents. We knew he would be fine and as soon as things settled down, we were bringing our son home. Due to his absence, I had to cancel his upcoming appointments. I called the office explained the situation and cancelled all but one appointment.

I was about five months pregnant and the doctor tells us based on certain test results that we needed to travel to UNC-Chapel Hill Hospital because there was likely something wrong with the baby. There were so many medical terms and so much to take in. My husband and I traveled to the neonatal specialist in UNC-Chapel Hill. We enjoyed our ride and kept our faith alive. I had seen stories of how those who had received the same news and beat the odds- they had healthy happy babies. Our son would not be any different. We arrived in Chapel Hill, faith in tow. Blood work was drawn, amniotic fluid was drawn and then it was time for the ultrasound. Our nurse became quiet. What was it? There was no heartbeat. Just like that. Nothing... We tried to ask questions but got no answers. We were sent straight back to my local doctor to get results and information. We rode back in silence with a few words in between. I don't recall shedding a tear. Even then I was afraid to cry. If I cried it would make it real. With all that was happening, I made one simple but life-altering oversight. With all that was going on, I simply it slipped my mind. I'd forgotten to cancel our son's appointment with the otolaryngologist.

I was admitted to the hospital. I did not accept what was happening. The doctor would induce my labor and I would have to deliver my stillborn son. There I was in the Labor and Delivery Unit. I was forced to feel the pain that should have translated into the appreciation of producing new life. Eating ice chips was supposed to soothe my nausea and curb my appetite, instead it reminded me of the coldness of death. Positioned as a heap in a hospital bed, drowned by the loud obliterating silence that should have been my baby's heartbeat. Waiting to push out the baby, the son that a spank on the bottom couldn't make cry. That was October 9, 1997, a Tuesday. I remember the day because the otolaryngologist's office only scheduled my son's appointments on Mondays. Mondays were my husband's days off and he would've been with me. Call it pregnancy brain or what have you but that day I forgot to cancel the appointment. I mean how was I expected to remember everything. Surely, they will understand, they are in the medical field. Emergencies happen on the regular. Sadly, I was mistaken and misinformed. I was in labor to deliver a stillborn, my active 2-year old was three states away at my in-laws living it up. What was I supposed to do? While in labor my phone rung-it was the otolaryngologist's office telling me that I had missed my son's second appointment and they would be forced to contact the department of social services. I handed the phone to someone and turned over. Everything concerning the phone call to this day a blur. I was in labor. Surrounded by family, trying to make the best of a devastating situation. Finally, after hours of emotional labor, I delivered Caleb Malik Robinson. His name was intentional, it means "King." He was cremated and the name plate placed. It was so very hard. I could not function. Until recently, I purposely blocked out the last quarter of that year. As a family, we tried to resume life as it once was. No matter how I tried, there was no normalcy. My husband was home for a short time before he had to return to work. There I was at home trying to get it together so that my son could come back home.

Not only was I hiding depression but I would not allow myself to grieve. It was almost as if I was smashing my foot on the brakes of a car. I can say now that I was afraid to grieve. Someone told me, "The Lord giveth and the Lord taketh away, blessed be the Name of the Lord." I said thank you, while screaming on the inside. "How dare you dress up this loss for me as if it is sanctioned and glorious?" I did not get rude, I did not go off. I just ended the conversation. The few months passed and I was on the mend. The doctor had prescribed me Zoloft, which was deemed the happy pill. Of course, I took it once and said, "I am not taking this medication, my faith is going to get me through this.

I don't need medication. My body is healed, my heart is healed, my emotions are healed in Jesus name." I pushed myself to keep going. My husband was on the road and would call daily to check on us. My oldest and I were doing just fine. No "happy pill", No therapy. Jesus was my doctor. Reality was, I still put on that smile. I still dressed up. Yet, at the end of the day, I wasn't sleeping well at night and when I did sleep my dreams were of losing Caleb and guilt was chasing me down. Somehow it was my fault that Caleb died. I woke up defeated. I went throughout the day defeated. I went to bed defeated. A maddening cycle that just wouldn't stop. As I attempted to just get through day to day routines-there were a few times that I would have to walk away and cry. Normal tasks such as doing my daughter's hair were challenging for me. The simplest things had me in a tizzy. Again, I wouldn't give myself permission to just be. I had to keep going.

In the midst of my "keep on keeping on," I was improving or so I thought. All was right with the world until late one night when there was a knock at my back door. I am totally confused. First, who comes to my home this time of the evening unexpected. Second, who comes to my back door. I looked outside and saw a Sheriff's deputy. My heart was racing. I couldn't help but wonder if something happened to my husband? Fear was raging, as I opened the door. Standing with the deputy was a little short lady from the county department of social services. She was there to investigate me based on reports made by the otolaryngologist's office. Just when I thought things could not have gotten any worse. The medical office, doctor and nurse had made claims of medical neglect against me. The summons alleged that I was medically neglect in caring for my son because we had missed appointments. His safety was in question. I looked at the summons. I looked from the worker to the deputy and from the deputy to the officer. I looked at the dates in question and the very thing I thought I had conquered, the very thing I thought I had suppressed to the point of no return was staring me in my face. I had never been in trouble with the law so anxiety was running a marathon around me and poking me like acupuncture needles. Instead of calming, it sent me into a nervous tizzy. All on the inside, though. I was silent and stuck in time until the worker shook me and called my name. She told me in a matter of fact tone that they had visited my home a few times and did not get an answer. Which was likely true, those months prior in dealing with losing my son were rough. I did not answer the door for anyone. If you didn't have a key you did not get in. Period. Because they knew I was in the home and not responding- they'd called the Sheriff's deputy to accompany her on this evening. If my son had been in the home and anything about him looked out of the norm, I would've been arrested and my children removed from the home. I was floored. I had to balance myself on the deep freezer. We were still at the back door. I did not let them come any further into my home. Yet, their presence violated me. I had go in my prayer closet, in a storage box. I had to bring out the urn that contained Caleb's ashes, his death certificate, my hospital records and wrist bands.

I had to show the notice from the doctor placing me on bedrest. Inside the box were his footprints, his hat, his wristband, t-shirt and blanket. The pain had been unearthed and there I was again. I was frozen in horrid dismay as they scanned documents, and looked through my Young King's box. How could this be happening? Not this, not now. But it was happening. I was then informed by the two officials that I had one week to produce my son or I would be arrested and charged. I saw sympathy on her face. She did not want to tell me that but she had a job to do. When they left, I called one of my neighbors from down the street. She came and sat with me to help me make heads of what was really happening. I could not wrap my mind around what was going on. I was numbed. My husband was working out of state, I could not drive nine hours and back to get my son. What was I going to do? I had been successful at ignoring depression and suppressing grief. That wall had crumbled yet again as I faced pending legal issues because of something out of my control. At this point I did call for support. The support I reached for was not for depression- it wasn't even for grief- it was for my current situation. I was angry, frustrated, and overwhelmed. All of this made me even more tired and I was just stuck.

Without all the minor details, my husband went to get my son and I took him to the department of social services so they could physically see that he was alive and well. He had to be checked for malnourishment and other indicators of abuse. Once that was over, I had to take him to the very doctor that made the accusations. Unbeknownst to me, the hospital, my ob-gyn and a few others had been in communication with this doctor. Letters were written on our behalf. By the time I arrived, they were catering to us. Truth is they were afraid we were going to sue them. The thought did cross my mind but at the end of the day-he was not my enemy. I was.

Reflecting on that incident, I realize how exhausted I was. I was so tired of fighting what I knew but did not want to admit. I was tired of smiling. I was tired of keeping on keeping on. But I did not know what else to do. I dared not be transparent because I wanted to avoid a sermon and scripture catalog. When you are enduring certain situations, a sermon is the last thing you want to hear. You don't want to hear quoted scriptures. You don't really want someone to reference God's role in what you are facing. No, none of that. You want to know why it happened, how it happened and who was going to fix whatever remained to be fixed.

Anxiety had opened the door for panic attacks and my insomnia worsened without warning. I gave up trying to explain it. So, what did I do? I kept on keeping on. Knowing that I was in a mess but because it wasn't addressed, I made myself believe I would be just fine *at some point*. There were people that felt sorry for me because of my loss. They could identify with death. But they couldn't identify with the heaviness of such an intimate loss.

Comforting words were spoken, but my pain screamed louder. The hugs were well meaning, but my numbness outweighed them. People were hugging me and loving on me because I had lost a child. They were loving on me because of the issue with department of social services. They were loving on me because that is what your support system does, they love on you. All while I was sinking deeper into depression. They assumed my blood shot eyes were from crying about my situation and not contributed to insomnia. There were times when I was without sleep for 30 hours. Yet, there it sat. Depression was still lingering like a dark cloud with a timeline of infinity. I did not know how to cope. I did not want to see the counselor. I did not want to take the meds. I wanted my faith to work. I wanted to be able to leave it on the altar and it would disappear out of my life. "God, you did it for so and so, what's so wrong with me that you won't do it like that for me?" I kept looking around pleading with God, "What is wrong with me, why won't You take this away from me? Why won't You cast it into the sea of forgetfulness?" "Why can't You blot it out like you've blotted out transgressions? Do I not know enough scripture, have I not prayed the right prayer, did not I miss giving You praise at some point of time? Did I miss a church service you intended for me to be a part of? Did I not sow enough into the offering?

God what is it, PLEASE TELL ME!!"

I was so set on portraying that I was living my best life that I ignored my depression. Ignoring my depression catapulted me into shuffling multiple faceted lives between grief and remembering who I was from day to day. I worshiped, I performed my duties as a wife and mother, and I was the go-getter and get it done girl for other areas of my life. The waves of torment and confusion were depression's breeding ground. I got plum tired. I kept up the masquerade party as long as my heart would allow. I spent years carrying the guilt of my son's death. Memories of the laborversary agonized me to the point of physical pain. My high blood pressure became worse. It was no longer a little thing. It was major. For years I could not drive by the otolaryngologist's office. Going anywhere near that route cause panic attacks that paralyzed me. Listen, let me tell you, I was a hot mess. I wanted to be okay but I was not. I wanted to be the same woman for me that I was for everyone else. But I was not. I was exhausted. Some moments I was so exhausted, I wanted to cry, I felt a cry, but the tears would not come. I was at a standstill and life was continuing around me like a whirlwind. During that time, the ministry we were a part had shut down. If we had been a part of a local church at that time church, I would have gladly submitted to counseling from my pastor.

It is wonderful when Pastors have counselling sessions with members. It is absolutely necessary because it affords a level of accountability   and opens   up   an   avenue   of communication. However, there are some things that a pastor may not be able to touch. Once again, I had been triggered. I had to tap in to the outside source of help- therapy. Professional therapy helps identify specifics and I was able to better target my prayers and those who were praying with me.

Going through these episodes is not something I should have ever tried to go at alone. My post-trauma exhaustion was leveled higher than that of just being tired. It was registered at the top of the Richter scale and at any moment everything that I had suppressed was at the brink of a volcanic eruption.

Prayer was vital in getting through my post-traumatic exhaustion. But I wasn't the one praying. I couldn't pray. Through my intense therapy sessions, one of the things I learned was that I needed a support circle. This support circle could not consist of those I had been supporting and in return expected support. This circle had been comprised of genuine people who were not afraid to deal with this me. Ones who could handle being a safe place for me to vent, cry, scream, and just release, without judgment. When I was finished doing whatever I needed to do, this person would hug me, and sometimes pray with me at that very moment.

Rest Stop 2.5

Okay let's stop for a moment. As I write this my tears are falling. I picture my troubled soul and wonder how many others have had similar seemingly unanswered conversations with God and felt like He had turned a deaf ear to us. He did not respond. The more you read, journal and pray, you will begin to understand that there are no identical journeys. Maybe you have not lost a child, or you lost a child in a different manner. Maybe you lost a spouse, sibling or just someone who was very close to you. Maybe you lost a marriage to divorce. Maybe you lost your dream job because of a mistake. Your loss is what you say it is to you. No one can tell you how to measure your loss. Your goal is to take one day at a time. One step at a time. One moment at a time. One breath at a time. Give yourself permission to take this journey, ridding yourself of guilt and blame.

Let's take a moment and I want you to reflect on a time in your life when deep down you wanted to deal with the depression and the grief but you did not know how. What situation or issue were you facing? Take a moment and be honest with yourself. This is you, your heart and your truth. Close your eyes, inhale, exhale and think.

Personal Declaration and Affirmation

Today, at this moment I give myself _____(name) permission to let it go. I vow not to even attempt to figure it all out today or any single day... I give myself permission to feel the pain that I was afraid of feeling because I didn't want to hurt anymore. But today, I commit to begin my healing. I have to uncover my wounds one at a time. I can't keep them bandaged because bandaged wounds without proper care, will become inhabited by bitterness which will in turn fester and thus create the environment for infections and deepen the sourness of my inner man. I am ready to deal with me. One small step at a time. Inhale - exhale – now go to your journal and Write.

Prayer

God, Almighty one and Most Righteous Father, I come to you on behalf of my dear friend reading this prayer. God, I know you knew us before we were formed and you know our story from the end to the beginning. Kind Sir, I pray now that you would grant relief for the person who is sick and tired of being tired. They are too tired to quit yet too tired to keep going. Exhaustion has shrouded them and they are stuck. We denounce every plan of the enemy over their lives. My sister needs your strength. My brother needs your strength. This thing is too much for them to handle but it's too painful to release without your help. God allow us to have a heart to forgive those who we thought were solids in our life and yet we were left alone and uncovered. God help us to release the prisoners of our hearts so that we can follow this journey to wholeness. God, we are tired of pretending, we are tired of simply existing. God, we are exhausted from trying to act as if everything is okay. Allow your comforter to be just that right now in the name of your son Jesus. God allow your grace to be the buffer we need in order to look beyond those things that have kept us from totality in times past. Thank you for allowing us to just breathe. Thank you for allowing us just to "be" in the safety of your presence. Thank you for hiding us behind your wings until we recover from whatever we are facing. We believe and declare that our new isn't coming. It is beginning now within us. Even if others do not see our growth, we shall be confident in your Word and take one step at a time. In your name we pray, Amen.

Mile Marker 3

Pressing Pressure and No Peace

"In peace, I will lie down and sleep, for you alone, Lord, make me dwell in safety." Psalm 4:8

I had a tendency to treat my day to day being and my emotional challenged being as two separate people. What do I mean? The day to day being is the us that gets up and puts on our best performance each day. We go to work and we have surface wins and gains that we place in the success column. The us that smiles and we earn the perfect score of A on our presentation. We are gift wrapped in shiny perfection and no one sees anything else. Then there is the other us. The us that's struggling with depression. The us that fights to wake up and live. The us that subconsciously sacrifices sleep because we are afraid of what our dreams/nightmares may reveal. The us that has to inhale and exhale as we countdown to avoid a panic attack. The us that gets to the church but you have to sit in the car and talk yourself into getting out because today is the day you just don't want to push anymore. The us that's in the local mall and all of a sudden you feel as if everyone is watching you. The sweat forms and the meltdown begins. Can I just tell you that some of the weight can be lifted if you just embrace that the part of you that's fighting in our emotions is NOT a separate being? This can help ease some of the pressure. Sometimes we often feel as if we have to choose who we will be from day to day. Is our accepted us strong enough to show up? Or is the struggling us going to be on deck for the daily performance? All pressure and no peace. You weren't created and labeled as two separate beings.

There is no perfect put together you and the other you. You are a whole being. I spent years and countless hours trying to mask the "other" me and keep it separate from the "accepted" me that my pressure was multiplied. When deep down inside I wanted to just "be." I just wanted peace.

We have all seen the wave of posts on social media telling people to check on their strong friend. You know the one who has it together enough that he or she is everything for everyone else? Yes, you know exactly which friend I am referring to, don't you? We follow the instructions and we check on that strong friend. As per usual, they will respond that they are okay and proceed to see how everyone else is doing. No matter what, it is an act of congress to get them open up about what's really going on with them. I am that person. I try not to rain on anyone's parade with my personal crisis. Yet, I am burdened with pressure and have little to no peace. I look peaceful, I act peaceful, I make peace but I have no peace. In the middle of the depression I was pressed.

My pressure wasn't coming from the outside it was abusing me with blows from the inside. I should have had my own personalized warning label. Contents Under Pressure. Anytime a container that houses flammable contents is under pressure from the outside it has the potential to catch fire and explode. What about when the pressure on the inside is pressurized and it bulging there is no give? You just walk around full of pressure and the absence of peace. The ironic thing about this is while nothing is being released from the pressure mass, something is always being added. Have you ever said, "God if one more thing happens, I am going to lose it?" That's pressure. I had moments where I was sitting on the edge of life's circumstances holding on for dear life because if the wind blew the slightest in my direction it was going to take me out of here.

Within the word 'depression' you see the word 'press'. It is not camouflaged nor is it scrambled. It's smack dab in the middle of the word. One of the meanings of the prefix 'de' is down to the bottom. Mishandled or not handled depression and ignoring the truth of what is going on stirs the recipe for a break down. How do I know? I know because I have been there on more than one occasion.

Let me ask, have you ever been under so much pressure that you could not physically move? Have you ever been in a place where you were so emotionally overwhelmed that you were physically crippled? Just so you know I can relate, I will share my story.

One day I was at work and everything was going

per usual. I was just busy with a little of this and a little of that. I am not sure how I got to this upcoming point but without a doubt, I was there. I sat up in my office chair, those bottled up tears started falling and I slid to my hands and knees. Thankfully, I'd made sure my door was locked before I sat down. I was down there for what seemed like an eternity. I grabbed my chest and I told God, that I needed an intervention. This was not a casual God I need you type moment. This was an urgent cry for supernatural, urgent, divine intervention. The pressure pounced on my chest like a ton of bricks. I did not have the strength to get up nor did I have the desire to stay on a cold, unforgiving cement floor. I pulled the desk phone to the floor and called the two extensions that I could remember. I thank God for my two angels even today. One came and pulled me off the floor into her arms. She hugged me in an attempt to ease the pain. Then we called the other angel. She checked my blood pressure and gave me some of the most precious words. They both spoke to me in such a way that I was granted instant calm and peace was returning in increments. That was perfectly fine with me because I knew without a doubt that it was coming.

I needed that peace right then more than anything in the world. They both convinced me to call my medical doctor. I was hesitant because a few weeks prior, my doctor was encouraging me to begin self-care immediately. My heart was in overdrive, blood pressure was not stable. My extremities were swelling. She said I needed to take some time off from work to rest my body and rest my mind. Me, being the overachiever that I was proceeded to give my doctor a running list as to why I could not take the time off. What I did not realize was that she saw something brewing within me that I subconsciously ignored day in and day out. The pressure was building like a locked pressure cooker.

The ingredients had reached the top and there was no simmering it down. The heat somehow had been turned on high and it was a wrap. No one can say what that one thing will be to tilt you to the edge, but I promise you will not care what it is once that pressure reaches the boiling point. It is a matter of why, how and what to do next. Don't you understand that when you don't deal with the real issues and you continue to ignore, avoid, and mask them- at some point you will lose control. What you thought was peace was actually eye of the hurricane formed tight and raring forward.

That day I lost control and it took God himself to get me to a place where I could function just to get out of bed from day to day. No part of me was responding. I was in physical trauma and deep depression. Yes, I can say it now.

Had you asked me then I would have shrugged my shoulders and said, "no" through my ongoing flow of tears. I knew I needed help, I needed peace, I needed to breathe. I relief from the pressure. I did not have the strength to do anything. I mustered up enough to have surface conversations with my family but other than that my conversations were at level zero.

When I did begin to answer the phone, I still tried to carry the facade of being okay. To sum it all up, I was under a whole heap of cemented pressure with not an ounce of peace in sight. By this time, I'd met with my doctor a few times since the grand fiasco. She had prescribed me with a low dose anti-depressant and asked me if I was seeing a therapist.

Unlike my pride in the first Mile Marker, I didn't fight seeking help. I reached out to someone I knew. This someone was dear and had known me for many years. I had no idea she was 'that' type of counselor. I must admit I was hesitant because of what we knew about each other. I quickly realized not only was she my safest option, but that I was also very glad that God sent me to her.

Rest Stop 3.5

As you have read a few of my mile marker events, you can see it wasn't all about being in the church or around those who attend church. This was my job, my livelihood, my bread and butter. Yes, I broke down right there on floor in a place where people looked to me to help bring them out of similar places. Have you ever been there? Write it down. Have you ever been crippled and unable to move? Write it down. Have you been so afraid of breaking down that you refused to slow down? Write it down. Pressure, where is the pressure coming from? What have you been avoiding dealing with that you suppressed and it translated into more pressure? Write it down. Shed tears, shake, be mad, or however else you want to feel. But you need to write this down. Please don't continue to ignore a brewing explosion. Explosions don't have specific names they only have casualties. We don't want to create casualties unaware. Let's rest our pen on the paper and begin to release. Do you need someone to talk to? Begin looking up Licensed Professional Counselors in your area. There are even some Counselors that conduct sessions through video chat or phone. Whatever your choice is, please just reach out and get what you need. Again, Jesus is the Great Counselor and He has blessed many to work in this field as an extension of His kind and loving hand.

Declaration and Affirmation:

I was created as an overcomer. The pressures of life that weigh me down will no longer have dominion over my mind, body or my soul. I declare and decree that I am fearfully and wonderfully made by the Almighty and I will no longer house pressure that aims to destroy who I am destined to be. I am destined to be free and free indeed.

Prayer

Precious and almighty God, we come to you once again standing in the gap between peace and chaos. God, we ask now that you would come in and ease the pressure that wills to destroy me. The pressure that I thought I could control God I need your guiding and powerful hand to take control and release the pressure. God if I release the pressure I could face years of guilt and shame. I need you to do this for me. Set my heart at peace. Set my mind at peace. Allow me to focus on only what you have ordained for my life. God, you are my safe place and I ask that you guide me to those resources I need in order to continue on this journey. I refuse to stay stuck in this place. I am determined to move forward. I release my troubled heart and weary soul unto Thee. In Jesus' Name, Amen.

Mile Marker 4

Rejection's Wrath

"Even if my father and mother abandon me, the Lord will hold me close." Psalm 27:10

Rejection means the dismissal of or non-acceptance. We can easily speak on rejecting items from a delivery, rejecting damaged goods from the grocery store or even rejecting something on behalf of someone else. When these items are returned to the sender, they are resold at for meager coins. The company just wants to get rid of the inventory. Right? Well, let me shift your thinking for a moment. What about when you are the improperly packaged item, when you are the bent and rusted cans from the supermarket shelf? You're the opened and unwanted package. How do you handle that? Rejection on a personal level stings like that of a thousand wasps in attack mode. It hurts and you might even flinch at the very thought of rejection.

Flinch and grimace away. But rejection is someone's every day truth. There is someone very close to you who feels as if maybe they are labeled as the black sheep in the family, on the team, or in the company. Just maybe they feel like nothing they ever do is good enough. We have often heard that, man's rejection is God's protection. Yes, that does hold true. And yet, while we do thank God for His protection, one doesn't feel so protected when you are in the belly of your battle, and you're drowning in hopelessness. Maybe that someone isn't a person close to you. That someone is possibly, you.

Rejection is silent cruelty that preys on unsuspecting, vulnerable persons without warning. Rejection is the one thing that we often refer to in this statement, "Talk about me, give me constructive criticism, even leave me on 'read' in our text conversations (every now and then, but please mam, please sir, don't reject me and throw me away as the person identified as the *unwanted*.

In many instances, depression is triggered by some form of rejection. Rejection that festers creates the mold of resentment. Regardless as to whether it was intentional or not- for the person fighting this battle, it is still rejection. Rejection stings and burrows into our being like that of a stubborn splinter, that refuses to be removed by usual measures.

August 1983 is a date that is permanently etched in my mind. The day I was checked out of school and welcomed home by an entourage of cars and people. My mother was in her bedroom. Only certain ones were allowed in and out of her space. People were hugging me with fake smiles plastered on their faces and well-intentioned words mixed with awkward pauses. I was a kid, I had no idea what was going on. I knew something wasn't right. But hey, I was just a kid. Then the news was shared, my dad had died. In my mind, "What do you mean dead, he's gone?" Of course- I'm a child and I was not adult enough to understand so I just went with the flow. We (they) made funeral preparations and I was just being myself, playful and rambunctious. Just as the days and nights-people came and went. Hugs, food, drinks, cards, flowers, big cars, Masons and Eastern Stars along with the police department. Dad worked for the police department. He was one heck of a mechanic and was applauded as such. I remember, at the funeral, I cried, I was a daddy's girl. The day of funeral came and went. For some time after that someone stayed with us to help mom. They say that children are resilient. We were expected to jump back into our normal routine of going to school and learning. That is exactly what I did. Life was different and there were some struggles but we kept going. I mean what choice did we have?

I remember finding out some time later how my father died. I relived the day he died all over again. The funeral did not mean the same any more. The awkward pauses and fake smiles were validated and here I was as a child accepting what I was told, don't ask any questions and let the adults handle the important stuff. As I became older and these events replayed in my mind, my question was, who was handling me while they were handling the grown-up stuff. I kept playing and doing as children did. Yet, deep down inside bitterness was rooting deep in my being.

Let me interject that my momma was and still is a superwoman to me. She took care of us and protected us then and continues to do so now. There are just some things we did not have access to that are available now.

Please understand, He wasn't perfect nor was he a heavenly angel. He was my living example of a knight in shining armor. I loved him and he loved me. I was his princess and he was my king. Yet, in an instant, without warning, he's gone. He didn't just die, he committed suicide. He took his life with what seemed little to no thought of anyone, not even me. There was no note there was no mutual good-bye. It was like a story with a terrible ending and the viewer demanding their money back. Only this time, there was no do over. It was finished. "Oh death, that was a detrimental blow." Here I remain with my father's wit, slick tongue, and his love for people and his ability to bring joy with his contagious laughter. Understand, the bottom line - he's my daddy.

I felt abandoned and rejected by the one person that was supposed to be there for me for me. Growing up seeing the relationships between fathers and daughters was difficult. I was smiling on the outside but asking, "Why couldn't I have that with my dad?" Then trying to fit in and be a part of someone's complete family was a chore I felt I had to do. I felt I had to have it.

I have heard stories of women who hate their fathers and refuse to have a relationship with them for various reasons. I hear and in my heart and think to myself, "At least he is still here, fix it." There are mothers I have seen deny the child the right to have a relationship with the fathers because of adult issues. I want to scream, "FIX IT.!!"

If I could, I would bring my father back and have an adult conversation with him from the heart of a child. I got tired of singing and or hearing songs, that mentioned seeing my father in heaven. I wasn't banking on it at all. As a matter of fact, when those songs were sung, my heart did a side-eye and my eyes rolled back to my neck. Since I could not have a conversation with my dad, I had to secure my healing by any means necessary. I decided to have a conversation with my father and pour out my heart. I was determined NOT to stop conversing with him until I felt better. I just needed to figure out how. No, I did not want to pray. Before I could pray I had to deal with this. No one ever told me I wasn't good enough but his untimely death, the method of departure and the obstacles I have had to face were my supporting evidence that I was not good enough. Reality is, I wanted to sit on his lap, and listen to him tell me how much he loved me. I wanted him to apologize and tell me it was an accident-that he did not mean it. I wanted to hear him say, "Wake up it's a bad dream." Yet, I accept that unfortunately, no matter how much I wished it to be so - none of those things were going to happen. Again, I digress to say, I had to admit and accept that there are no do overs in death. Anyway, back to this conversation. Just the thought of having the conversation made my heart pound. I would rethink and rehearse the conversation in my head for days but that was not enough. I had to be free. There is nothing worse than being in held in bondage by someone who was no longer living. This was something beyond my span of control. It took me some time and tears, but when I done, I was done.

As we continue this journey, you will find the things that have hindered you the most were the things that were beyond your span of your control. I did not push my dad to commit suicide. I had no role in that. And will not allow guilt to persuade me otherwise. Our issue is that rejection by death or in my case, rejection by suicide is a hard truth to accept because it's so personal. This is where our struggle begins. In an effort to move forward we struggle with validation or the lack thereof. We struggle with not being accepted. We struggle with not having the energy to boost ourselves therefore, when the cheers stop so do we. Let's be honest, as we struggle we begin to rethink and reevaluate every relationship in our lives, while we are trying to forget about that one. The one that broke us.

I remembered the day, I shook myself from the grip of rejection. I was not at a church service. No one tarried with me. I was home alone. I stood in the bathroom mirror expressing that I was tired of holding on to a pain that I did nothing to deserve. I cried, I wept, I grabbed my chest until I was literally sick to my stomach. I got myself together (or so I thought) I went for a walk in the neighborhood. It was raining so my tears wouldn't be a distraction. As I lapped the neighborhood for the second time I headed back home to check the mail and go inside. It wasn't until I began to go through the mail that I got the idea to write my father a letter. Yeah, initially I was thinking, what is the point of writing him a letter, he's dead he can't read it. He's not going to respond in writing so what is the use. Writing the letter kept nagging at me. I finally agreed and penned, the first of many letters to my father. These letters were instrumental in setting me free. I was sick of feeling like a misplaced foster child. I was sick of the torment of his absence. I was more than ready this time. I could not let this disrespectful wrath of rejection be the end of me. Choosing to write this letter, was my first step to freedom.

Excerpt from, "Letters to My Father"

Hey Dad, I know it has been a while. I still miss you the same, I just chose to sort of deal with in my own way. I drove to your grave site and swept the straw from your marker. I just needed to see your name one more time. You know you have some grandchildren, great grandchildren and great-great grandchildren. I've been meaning to write this for some time now but the pain was too real and I just couldn't stomach penning the term "Dad." Listen sir, you know you did a real doozy on me, right? You woke us up and gathered us together and asked momma to pray. Yeah, you set us up for the Okie doke. Next thing I know you are gone. Okay, enough of the small talk. What was so bad that you had to leave me in such a disruptive manner? Yes, I get my straight shooter tendencies from you too. Dad, it has been a rough road. I wanted to give up so many times because you were not here. I did not have a daddy to call in troublesome times. Do you know how many times I turned my head to hide the tears, when I heard someone say, "Ima tell my daddy?" Who was I supposed to tell? You left me and the void has grown over the years like a cancer. Were you sick, oh wait you didn't want to tell us? Were you drowning in debt? You left me fatherless. I felt like a bastard. Excuse my French but it is in the Bible. You left me to figure out things on my own that I should've never had to think about. I spent years trying to process the rhyme and reason of why. Many nights I would wonder why wasn't I good enough for you to stay around. There were things you were supposed to teach me things that only a father can teach his daughter. You were supposed to teach me how to ride a bike and drive the little white car you bought for momma. You were supposed to scare my first boyfriend, cheer me on for graduation and walk me down the aisle to be married. You were supposed show me how to change a tire and change the oil. Instead you made the decision that whatever was going on, was carried more weight than your remaining with us for a lifetime. You carefully planned your day, and when you decided you were done, you made an intentional and untimely exit.

How could you set us up like that? How could act as if it was just another day, when you knew in your mind you weren't coming home? Or did you know? If I had known, I'd wiped the sleep out of my eyes and gotten a better look at your face. If I had known, I'd have hugged you a little bit tighter and not let you go so quickly. If I had known, I would have asked you to take the day off so we could've had our last father daughter day out for ice cream and fun shenanigans that only you could come up with. I'm telling you, you really created a mess here for me. You didn't have to, but you did.

Yea, you probably didn't think about that part. You probably said, momma would pick up the pieces, and granted she did. But, doggonit it did not have to be this way.

On that last day, you took more than just your life. You took a part of mine. You took my hope. You took away possibilities that I may never ever know about. You took it all, and you did it without the decency to say good-bye.

The letter continued for several more pages, I won't share the remaining parts of the letter because the meat of my letter to my father is not the point. The point was, I had to deal with how I felt. I had to deal with the unforgiving part of me that felt entitled to hold a grudge. With this letter, I sat and read it several times over. I read it out loud so I could feel rejection fighting the release of strength. I had used so much energy nursing the rejection that I was at ground zero with life. Rejection had worn me down to the point that I felt I wasn't any good for anyone. My father was dead, he wasn't coming back. Yet, in order for me to move forward- I had to dismantle rejection from its position of dominance within. I had to choose to forgive him. Forgive him for not wanting to love me more than he wanted to leave me. Forgive him for not teaching me all the things a father should teach his daughter. Forgive him for giving up instead fighting for us. Forgive him for making my momma work so hard as a single parent. Forgive him without an apology. Just forgive him. At the close of the letter, I wrote in red pen, "Daddy, I forgive you." With tears streaming down my face I re-read that letter until a release came. Finally, I could breathe.

Rejection will have you feeling all sorts of ways. Again, you will begin to randomly question every relationship in your life. My father's suicide had kidnapped me into a world of never having enough or never being good enough. I spent years trying to overcompensate to prove I was worthy of a friendship or relationship. I wasted so much money trying to buy my permanent spot in friendships or relationships that I was never meant stay in. Running a marathon to please people I thought I should have been connected with and wearing myself out. Only to be discarded like recycled bath water. Listen!! Rejection is a merciless antagonizer. And I, the victim of its cruelty, kept it empowered because I was afraid to be honest with myself and with others about where I was and what I was up against.

When I began to release and pray, I realized that this was not my portion of righteous living. I got a grip and a glimpse of my Jeremiah 29:11 life. Even though I did not know the plan, I knew without a doubt that there was a plan. I did not know what it would take but I knew it had to be something more than this. I wanted and needed to be rid of the weight of rejection. I ask you, "How bad do you want to be rid of it?"

Unlike some people, I will not say that I cried my last tear over this. I cannot honestly say that and mean it. Why? Because it was a significant loss and he is my father. The little girl in me will always remember and hold him dear. I will miss him. I will never erase him and conduct myself as if he never existed. Because frankly without him there would be no me. I owe him that regard and honor. What I no longer bear is the burden of feeling rejected, abandoned, unwanted and orphaned because of his suicide.

Rest Stop 4.5

Time to get up and stretch and take a break. You've been reading on this stretch of your journey for a minute. As you are breaking, take the time to think about where you find yourself in the rejection juncture. What significant person or people in your life intentionally or unintentionally rejected you? Who do you feel pushed you off as a stray and left you to fend for yourself? Is that person still living or deceased? Are you still in a superficial relationship with them? Are there things you need to say, that you have been afraid to utter with your lips? Yes, I want you to answer these questions one by one. You may ask why? You need this release so that you will be completely whole. I am asking you not to skip any questions that make you uncomfortable. I am asking that if you get to a question that makes you uncomfortable, stop, rest your pen and whisper a prayer for strength. We all encounter things that we are not particularly fond of for one reason or another. But, we cannot keep running from it. Please hear my heart on this. If we continue to run away from our issue and not face it head on, we will find ourselves on the hamster wheel of life. We will continue doing the same things we have always done, and for some reason expect different results. From my studies, I was taught that as the definition of insanity. Come on, take a step to confront the very feeling that has held you captive for what seems like an eternity. After you've answered the questions, I need you to start penning a letter or a note to whomever. Say your peace. ALL OF IT. Don't leave one thing out. Because this time, it's a done deal. We don't want to revisit this ever again. There is no page length requirement. Just write. Write and pray, pray and write. Once you feel your release, then shred the letter. Nope, don't ball it up and discard it. Shred the letter. If you ball it up you may be tempted to dig it out and erase, reword and ultimately end up back at square one. Now if the person is living you may desire to follow the same process. Remember, step by step, okay. You may write the letter and mail it to them, or simply ask to have a long overdue conversation. Take heed, that when you make this step, their response is NOT I repeat, IS NOT your responsibility or weight to carry. Your only objective is your release, freedom and the self-given permission to move forward from this once and for all. This process may take a little bit longer than the previous ones. It is perfectly fine. There is no rush. Remember, we are not in the business of overnighting or speeding through this journey.

Prayer

Dear Heavenly Father, I thank you for exposing rejection's hold in my life. Thank you for allowing me to feel your acceptance and embrace the fact that you love me unconditionally. Father, I believe you and take you at your word that You will never leave me nor forsake me and for that I am eternally grateful. Lord help me to forgive without the apology. Help me not to give my pride free reign in this situation and hinder my breakthrough. God, I pray that you would redeem the time that I have lost holding on this ONE thing, ONE person. I surrender this feeling of not being wanted to you and I embrace your love. As I take this step towards wholeness, I pray that you would allow me to have the courage I need to release and break the cycle of the repetitive struggle with rejection. You created me, you love me, and you will never walk out on me. For that I say thank you. I pray these things in Jesus' Holy and righteous Name. Amen

Mile Marker 5

Echo of Emptiness

For the sake of Christ, then, I am content with weaknesses, insults, hardships, persecutions, and calamities. For when I am weak, then I am strong. 2 Corinthians 12:10

Have you ever walked into a vacant home? I mean totally vacant. No furniture, appliances, wall décor nothing just empty. When you speak the sound waves of the spoken voice bounce off the walls, floor, and the ceilings. The hollow, yet deep sound produced and that sound is called an "echo." It doesn't matter which way you turn the echo remains. The echo does not cease until the owner begins to fill the home with the furniture and appliances.

When you begin furnishing a home, most people are very particular about the style, color, and size of the furniture. The placing is meticulous and rooms are rearranged more times that one can count. Oftentimes we are just like that vacant home, empty. We make attempts to fill it with things. Materialistic personal items such as high-end fashion pieces of clothing, shoes and accessories. We spend money on top of the line vehicles and houses in neighborhoods we very well may not be able to afford. What makes us do these things? What makes us spend frivolously and waste money on unnecessary things? I am glad you asked. It is the emptiness that is housed on the inside that drives us to continuously make spontaneous and more than often, emotional purchases. Once the glam of the purchase is over, everyone has adored your new things and yet here you are again with a house, garage, or closet full of "stuff" you are still empty and the echo just gets louder and louder. The echo is resounding louder and louder. You can't drown it out nor can you ignore it. Please, take a seat and listen to my interlude of echoing emptiness.

My husband and I married young. He was twenty-five years young and I was twenty-two. I had my daughter and we were expecting our son. With all that was going on, we jumped into marriage, blind with no idea of what was to come. We were living for the Lord and going on with God anyhow. We were faithful to each other and to God. Somewhere stored in the back of my mind I had a hidden list of unspoken but desired expectations. God knew, but it was known to God and God alone. And frankly, according to my mindset, it wasn't anyone else's business. Yes, that is exactly what I said. I was a good wife with good intentions and a dash of extra expectations of which my husband was unaware. No, there were not hidden agendas, just a list of expectations that when I look back on them now, were unrealistic.

My husband was doing an awesome job of taking care of our family. I was not working in the beginning and he carried the load of responsibility without question or reservation. (Thank you, Honey) We worshipped together, we prayed together, we lived and enjoyed life together. You know, I mean at the beginning of marriages it is supposed to resemble a fairytale, right? Wrong! We had begun to bicker and argue. I was feeling some type of way about something at least every other day. This was a consequence of my "other" list on reserve. I did not verbally articulate anything but with red ink I was making mental notes of things to tap into and remember. I was always finding something to complain about. It was either what he was doing or what he wasn't doing. If he was doing something but not doing it the way I liked. Then I would turn around and expect him to pamper me and wipe away the woes of the day. Man, I am laughing now just thinking of how silly I was when got married. Well, when he would not respond to my complaints and or not do what I requested I disappeared into a self-willed depression. Self-willed, meaning I thought of things that would trigger me to a downward spiral. I watched things on television that fed into my darkness. After a few days, I would go into my prayer area and plead to God for help. Reason being is that after I self-willed myself into that pit, I could not self- will myself out of it. Yes, it was that serious This unhealthy behavior continued for years into our marriage. I had 99 problems and him leaving me was not one of them, so I inadvertently took his dedication and commitment for granted. Nevertheless, as the years progress the behavior became toxic. Not for our marriage alone but even more so for me the woman. Several years had passed and we were on the up and up so to speak. I was not creating habitual negative behaviors as often. You're probably saying, what in the world does this have to do with the echo of emptiness. Keep reading...

I wanted his undivided attention. I wanted to chat with him several times a day and talk him to death when he arrived home after enduring a workday of twelve to fifteen hours. Yeah - I know, I know a sad state of affairs.

After about ten years of marriage, I was in my prayer room on my knees. God spoke to me clear as the day is long. It made me shiver and sit at attention. "Vanessa, STOP IT!" I looked dumbfounded. I may have looked crazy but the He continued speaking. "Your husband is not your father. Stop expecting him to fill that gaping hole. Stop expecting your husband to fill a void that was never meant for him to fill. The place you are trying to make him fit is for me and me alone." "If you would put more time into getting closer to me minus your personal agenda for your unsuspecting husband, then you wouldn't have such turmoil within." There I was minding my business, doing my devotion and giving God what I thought was His due diligence and I was rebuked by GOD himself. That rebuke felt like a spanking I had receiving after my grandma ran the switches through the water. OUCH!!!

It was at the point that I realized, I had to allow God to sit in His rightful position which is the center of my life. I was so dead set on getting all of the gains from my husband- I totally ignored God except when it was convenient for me. I am being totally honest.

As I began to dissect and understand what God meant the tears fell and I was repentant. Remember in the previous chapter I'd lost my father, correct? Well, I did not know that I was expecting my husband to fulfill the role as father AND husband. That in and of itself was a startling reality. I was empty and the space was widening. Me and my selfish self was determined to force my husband into a role that did not belong to him. And God is a jealous God. I had to repent, apologize and regroup. I wanted him to fill the emptiness imposed by my father's absence. I wanted him to see the need of a fatherless little girl and still love me as his wife, the woman he married. Without him willing to assume that role in my life I was constantly reminded of my state of emptiness and the repetitive echo.

You will probably say, Vanessa, I did not do that to my husband. Okay, maybe not. Remember, there are no cookie cutter journeys. Maybe it was a relationship with a different relative, a long-time friend, spiritual mentor or advisor. When they did not come through to meet your expectations, you felt betrayed, empty and broken. You kept a running scoresheet on the tablet of your heart. After each "experience" someone else always won. You were never the winner. You heard the announcement bounce off the walls of your empty space, "Them - 1 You - 0." Yet, instead of dealing with your misappropriation of placement in your life you found yourself re-entering the blame game day in and day out- sometimes several times a day. Each time you were aware of what was going on, you found it easier to suffer alone, remain empty and act as if all was right with your world while you continued to blame everyone, for every disappointment in your life.

One of the primary reasons, I ended up in this predicament was due to my rose-colored glasses. Yes, I took so much time looking at other people's marriages. I wanted what I thought they had. I wanted what looked like relationship perfection. What I did not know was the "hell" many of those relationships were in the midst of. Yes, I envied in other people what I did not have. I had no idea what was on the other side of the wall of pretense.

Now, let me expose these hard truths to you- just

in case you still don't get it

1. You are upset with them for not doing something that they were never supposed to do. Does this make any sense at all? I'll explain, no worries. In my marriage, the more I tried to force my husband in God's place in my life and home were full of tension. He was trying to figure out why I was feeling some type of way. I was upset and argumentative because he was not attentive enough as to why I was feeling some type of way. He was not reading my mind and I was upset. Totally senseless, right? But during that time, I was convinced that I was justified and deserved immediate vindication and gratification. Yes, that is my truth.

2. You are living in a self-created victimization. Before you get mad and close the book, just listen- I am saying this is because it is exactly what I was doing. It was a classic case of "Woe is me." I would magnify on what was not happening (going my way) and who was allegedly causing me grief (my husband). I was capitalizing on my "weaker vessel" mentality which I used

at my convenience (to bring attention to what I wanted).

Maybe your expectations weren't from a spouse. Maybe it was from a friendship. You know the friend you call "sissy?" Or your 'bff' only they did not know they were your 'bff.' Or they knew they were you bff but did not reciprocate how you treated them. I understand that exposing this place makes us feel very vulnerable. We repeat this phrase in our heads, while fighting back tears. "I ain't no punk." I am not calling you a punk, you're just removing a layer in your heart that you thought would be there forever. Just think the longer a bandage stays on your skin, the glue begins to mesh with you skin. It attaches to those fine hairs of your arms and grips for dear life. Precious, it's time to remove the bandage and let your skin breathe.

Emptiness is a cantankerous bleed, that can be the cause of depression OR the result of depression. Through those years, my husband was clueless. I only shared what I wanted him to know and I expected him to figure the rest out. Yes, again I wanted him to read my mind. Totally, unfair. The one time I opened up to him, he wasn't prepared and when I mentioned depression, his response was not what I wanted and it angered me more. For various reasons, he could not understand what it was. Mainly, because he was so over me and my behavior he did not even try.

After a while, I knew I had created a mess, and only God himself could get me out. This problem was that I only wanted him to deal with the part I wanted him to deal with. Wrong. Wrong. Wrong. Half-heartedly submitting to the will of God only created deeper emptiness and a messed-up situation.

After trying to do it my way, I finally accepted something had to change. No, someone had to change. And that someone was me. I finally invited my husband to attend some of my therapy sessions. Not for him. For me. I needed him to understand what I was facing and how my day to day life was affected. Those first sessions were a doozy. He would try to take in all that was going on as best he could. When we got in the car, he bombarded me so many questions. Yes, I was prescribed medication. No, I did not take like I was supposed to. I just wasn't ready. As time progressed, I opened up to my husband some more. I had to take ownership of a lot of my actions that were not so good. I had to check my behavior and realign my relationship with God before I expected my relationship with my husband to improve.

Life continued and opposition presented itself. The only difference was that where I was once empty was being filled. I started doing things that were bringing me joy. I was reading and writing for myself. I continued going to sessions, but this time around, I was ready. I went with questions, notes, and honesty.

Rest Stop 5.5

Well, that was a doozy. I am thankful we have arrived at the rest area. You need a break. I need a break. WOOSAH...

Let me apologize to you from you. I apologize that you felt it was okay to remain empty and unfulfilled all these years. I apologize that you are so accustomed to the emptiness that you are clueless as to how to have a fulfilled life. I am terribly sorry, from you to you that you have run in circles trying to fill a void with a person when in reality, it was not nor will it ever be their rightful place. It's time to silence this echo and get you moving forward.

Take a moment and ponder. This part you cannot rush through. Take your time to answer each of these questions from the perspective of embracing the truth so that we won't create a cycle of this behavior. Who have you been disappointed by because of your unmet, unknown expectations? How did this make you feel? Did you cut that person off? Did you begin to treat them differently? Have you isolated yourself because you've blamed others for disappointing you? Do you measure other relationships in your life by the disappointment?

Make sure you write your responses down. Write

them down so when you pray you can see them and release them at the foot of the cross. Yes, I know some of the answers are going to be difficult to pen and even more difficult to speak aloud when you pray. But, it is not the end. It is the opening up for your beginning. You don't have to remain empty.

Prayer

Dear Heavenly Father, Thank you for the opportunity to come into your presence and rest on your wings of safety. Thank you for granting me the push I need to continue on this journey. The journey is uncomfortable and challenging but Lord I am determined to see it through. Now Lord, I release every person in my life from my hidden agenda and disappointment. God forgive me for having these extensive standards to make them priority in my life and me in theirs. When the truth is, that place in my life belongs to you and you alone. Lord heal my heart from my self-induced victimization. Lord I don't want to be empty and frustrated about being empty. God, I need you to come in and fill up every empty space in my life. God, I choose on today silence the hollow sound of the echo and replace it with worship and adoration towards you. God, I am aware that you are a jealous God, but you are not a forceful God. With that being said, God I give you permission to reside as the center of my life. I give you permission to take your rightful place in my life. Forgive me for even considering giving a physical person Your place, simply because I can see and touch them. From this day forward, my relationship with you takes priority. I will embrace and honor who you are in my life. In Jesus' Name, Amen.

Mile Marker 6

Self-Sabotage

"That the God of our Lord Jesus Christ, the Father of glory, may give unto you the spirit of wisdom and revelation in the knowledge of him: The eyes of your understanding being enlightened; that ye may know what is the hope of his calling, and what the riches of the glory of his inheritance in the saints",

Ephesians 1:17-18

The term sabotage is synonymous for destruction. Self is the nominative directed towards one's individual self. Self-sabotage- destruction of one's self.

Teenagers should be classified as an exclusive species. Adults who were once teenagers, will silently agree. Teenage years can be the most exciting, daring and determining years of one's life. My teenage years brought many unexpected events that changed my perspective on life.

In a previous chapter, I shared that my father committed suicide in August 1983. At that time, I was the tender age of ten years old. In August 1988, I decided that since, my daddy took his own life, then I should follow his steps and take my own life. I wasn't fitting in in school. I was struggling in my classes. I couldn't seem to do anything right.

I woke up one morning earlier than usual. I walked into the kitchen and took out every pill bottle I could find. I stood there and just started chucking pills. I took a drink of vinegar to wash them down and I repeated this until I figured I'd taken enough. I went on to get ready for school. By my calculations I should've passed out and sleeping my way into eternity within a few hours. This time span included my ride with mom to the home where I caught the bus and the wait for the bus to come. I would load the bus and at some point, I would die at school. I would die in faces of those who criticized and made fun of me. I would die in front of those who made me feel less than accepted. At 15, I was tired of living. Tired of trying and not yielding the peace I needed just to attend class in a junior high school.

We rode in the car and the pills did not want to stay down. My mom was driving and before we could out of the neighborhood, I was regurgitating. Mom did not know what to think. I wasn't thinking at all. I stared blankly and endured the ride. My mom was a single parent and her position at work was not one she could just take off work. She dropped me off at the house where I would get on the bus. I went in the house and I became sicker. I struggled keeping it together. I wanted everything to end at the school house. The longer I fought, the sicker I got. I sat at the kitchen table and I put my head down. I looked up and from somewhere I heard, dial 9-1-1. Me, calling 9-1-1 was not a part of my plan. I kept hearing, dial 9-1-1. I looked up and I saw a vision of Mother Armanda Murphy. She was my childhood pastor who had since passed on. I saw her sitting in her chair in her living room, she said, "Nessa, you are gonna live, baby. It is not your time to die. You have too much to do." Tears streaming down my face, I nodded and said, "yes mam." It was then that I picked up the phone, I called 9-1-1 and then I called my Godmother Betty. I was terrified. I did not want to live but by then I did not want to die.

Suicide is probably one of the highest physical representations of self-sabotage. At the age of fifteen, I was battling depression and had no idea what it was or how I got there.

Later in life, I learned that I was not healed from the trauma of losing my father. My mother did the best she could to get me the help I needed, but even then, I wasn't too keen on opening up to strangers.

I am so thankful that I did not succeed in taking my own life. But for the grace of the Almighty God. Had depression had its way, I would not be here writing to you.

Fast forward into adulthood. In many areas of my life I felt like the black sheep. I felt as if I was not good enough. I was not allowed to succeed. I was not allowed to have gains. The only thing I deserved to do was lose. During the moments when I came close to winning, I purposely doubled back just so I could take myself out of the running. Why did I do this? I did it because if I removed myself from almost winning, I would spare myself from the disappointment of not winning. I consistently lived this defeated life for many years.

My heart couldn't take another blow. I couldn't stomach another loss and I was already teeter tottering on the edge each and every day. It would've taken a feather of a blow to knock me to the edge of no return.

I can't count the number of times I was so bent out of shape with life and while driving down the road, I would think about how I could veer into oncoming traffic and it would not look like suicide. There were nights when I prayed God don't let me wake up, only to open my eyes and cry because I woke up. I did not think I could endure anything else life had to offer. Self-sabotage- I destroyed what could have been just in case it would not yield success.

I came to know what imposter syndrome was and how I was a textbook case. I laughed when I realized this because had I known I was a candidate to be a textbook case I would have found a reason not to do it.

During these times, I was still attending church, active in ministry, encouraging others and doing whatever I could do to support the ministry. I prayed about everything BUT what I was dealing with. I encouraged others to follow their treatment plans and ignored my own.

Yes, I had a treatment plan. My therapist made

sure I had one and understood what I was do in order to comply. I just did not listen.

My treatment plan included: taking my medication, eating right, reading, journaling, writing, getting enough rest, doing things that brought me joy, and exercising. I was to avoid anything that would trigger a relapse. Anything that would cause me to spiral backward or lower-I had to avoid it. My therapist was very thorough in planning with me. I even attended some mindfulness workshop sessions. Having all these things in place was lovely, except I was not doing what I was supposed to do.

Taking medication was hard for me. I was so caught up on what would people think if they found out. Now I am not saying everyone needs medications for depression. I am telling you what I needed until I could get to a place where I no longer had such a massive chemical imbalance.

Again, self-sabotage. Me not following my treatment plan because pride wouldn't let me, was self-sabotage. Me remaining connected to people who seeped toxicity in life, was self-sabotage. So many of us suffer from the weighted garment of self-sabotage. It gets to the point where we are enthralled with not succeeding that we default to self-sabotage without even thinking about it.

Some Years ago, my pastor, Pastor Delia Jenkins, preached a sermon, "From Suicide Watch to Purpose." This message literally saved my life and pulled me back on track. I was on suicide watch and had no idea what that meant at the time. I knew what it was but I did not know what it meant as it applied to me. I was indeed on the verge of aborting everything that was leading me to purpose. But on this Sunday Morning she delivered the word that served as a defibrillator. Your words brought me back to where I could have an honest conversation with God. It was after then, that I asked God to take away the blanket of self-sabotage, I did not understand what I was asking. I was not killing myself physically but I was killing who God wanted me to be because I was afraid of not measuring up. I asked God to teach me how to release the fear of succeeding that caused me to attempt to destroy what was meant to be a part of my life. I asked God to help me not to compare myself to others and feel intimidated by the unequal measurements. After all, comparison kills. It was killing me softly and I was ready to live.

I began reciting scriptures daily, several times a day, to affirm who I was in God and who He was in my life. I would post them in my office at work, in my office at home, in my bedroom beside my bed, in my bathroom on the mirror and many other places. I was just regaining my footing and I needed all of the reinforcements I could get. As I grew in my faith those scriptures were embedded in my heart and rolled from my mouth by memory. The God of peace restored me and I am so thankful for His mercy.

Rest Stop 6.5

It has been quite the ride through these last few chapters and breaks are always welcome. As I was writing these chapters, I began to look forward to the pit stops like a childhood nap time. (smile)

This Pit Stop is going to hit different. I want you to deal with the part of you that has been unintentionally sabotaging the things that were destined to push you forward. I want you to denounce that sabotaging vagabond spirit and give yourself permission to move forward. During this pit stop you are going to denounce fear. The root of self-sabotage is fear. One of the well-known acronymic phrases for fear is: False-Evidences-Appearing-Real. Fear is an illusion and you are not a failure.

Once you've gathered yourself enough to do that, then I want you to note the areas in YOUR life that YOU know you have sabotaged. I want you to be specific. Do you sabotage relationships because you don't feel you deserve to be loved?
Do you sabotage your career opportunities because you are afraid you might fail? Do you sabotage dreams and visions you were given about entrepreneurship because you are afraid to fail? Those are just examples. There are many other areas where we can sabotage. Once you have

pinpointed these sabotaged areas- repent. Pray and ask God to show you how to move forward and not repeat the same behavior.

Prayer

Dear God, we come to you with these things that we have fallen prey to. We come to you asking you to help rid us of the cycle of self-sabotage. Forgive us for our destructive behavior and allow us grace to do better. Help us to apply your Word to the areas where we are vulnerable. Lord, I declare I won't feel guilty for taking medication anymore. I won't be ashamed of getting the help that I need. Lead me in the right direction. I will no longer lean to my own understanding. But God, I will acknowledge you. I need you. I trust you to lead me to where you want me to be at this point in my life. I relinquish control totally and surrender to your will. Thank you for the opportunity to grow from where I am and into the place where you want to use me. In Jesus' Name, Amen

Mile Marker 7

Sanity and Safety

"What then shall we say to these things? If God be for us, who can be against us?"
Romans 8:31

Within the past six chapters I have shared about some of the events in my life that triggered some things in me that I did not necessarily think I needed at that particular time in life. However, everything that I have shared, I endured it, I survived it and I know am better because of it.

When faced with depression, whether you have an official diagnosis or not- the experience alone will have you questioning two very specific things about yourself. Those two things are your sanity and your identity.

Sanity is defined as the ability to think and behave in a normal and rational manner having sound mental health. I promise you with all the things I have shared with you and some of the things I did not share, I had come to believe that my sanity had been sidelined. Not only was I depressed, but I was on the verge of losing my mind. I couldn't process things correctly, I was repeating things that I did not think I heard clearly. Things became garbled together and sometimes I had to write things down before I could understand. This went on for such a long time. There were times when I was driving and would go into a daze and end up somewhere I did not intend to go. I was so caught up in thinking about the trauma that caused my depression and trying to figure out how someone like me got to the place where I was.

I am a dreamer and even in my dreams I was tortured. I would have dreams where I was running only to look and find myself in the same spot. Sweaty, thirsty, and out of breath in the same spot. In my dreams depression had a face and it was either trying to drown me or strangle me.

I woke up tired and really thinking I was losing it. I went right back to the scripture that talks about keeping our minds in perfect peace. Listen, I've quoted, recited, preached, and dissected that scripture I knew it when I did not think I knew it. But when your mind is tested and that is the only scripture that grants you peace, then you know that you don't only know it, but you have applied it. I actually recorded myself reciting this scripture on my voice recorder from several different bible versions. Why? Because when sleep would not come and my mind would not settle down, I would listen to this scripture until I fell asleep. This practice may sound elementary to some, but it is what worked for me. In hearing the scriptures and positive affirmations-I was able to push through. It was not a quick fix, but it was a practice I used in between therapy sessions, bible study and Sunday worship services.

It is quoted in scripture, "Thou will keep him in

perfect peace whose mind is stayed on thee." When my mind began to wander and I found myself going into a dark place, this scripture was my saving grace. I could not really express what I was feeling outside of therapy. My support circle knew when I called and just said a quiet hello- I needed support.

Make sure you trust your support circle enough to be transparent with them and be safe. Sanity and safety go hand in hand. Encountering incidents that cause you to question things that you should be otherwise be certain about requires you to have strategies and interventions in place. It is okay not to be okay. What is not okay is not acknowledging you're not okay and living a continuously lie. As you've read in previous chapters, the strategies of avoiding and ignoring were useless and dangerous.

Protect your sanity, ensure your safety, and secure your peace.

Mile Marker 8

Identity

"Accept one another, then, just as Christ accepted you, in order to bring praise to God."

Romans 15:7

Identity is the way you think about yourself, the way you are viewed by the world and the characteristics that define you. When addressing my identity, I realize I did not have one. I was so focused on what others thought about me and having them to validate me that I did not know who I was. Vanessa was somewhere lost in the shuffle. As you are traveling through this journey, find out who you are. Embrace who you are. If there is something you don't like, change it because you want to, not based on what someone else says. Be true to who you are and don't let opinions of other define you. Live your life according the promises spoken over your life. Yes, I know struggling through depression it is almost certain that you will have an identity crisis. I agree, I had an identity crisis. I just didn't stay there. I couldn't stay there. And neither will you when you make up in your mind to be who you were destined to me no matter the odds you face.

Mile Marker 9

Opposition

"Some trust in chariots and some in horses but we will trust in the name of the Lord our God."
Psalms 20:7

Opposition is present throughout the entire journey. As soon as you feel as if you have a leg up, then something else comes and knocks you back to where you thought you were delivered from. Some of the things we view as opposition we may find that they are tools for the journey. This is where you dig your heels into purpose and keep going. Yes, I was diagnosed with Chronic Depressive Disorder. Yes, I had to take medication for a while. Yes, I had to attend therapy for

several months (thankful for insurance). Yes, I had to step from some things that were overwhelming me. Yes, yes, yes, and yes. I said all that to say that opposition pushed me to grasp these resources and get myself in line.

Mile Marker 10

Never-Now-Next

*"Being confident in this one thing, that He who
began a good work in you will carry it on to
completion until the day of Christ Jesus."*
Philippians 1:4

Never let anyone tell you, you lack faith because you are on medication for depression or any other emotional challenges. Depression is a condition and for some people medication is the only thing that keeps them grounded. This does not mean they lack faith. I wouldn't dare tell someone who is on blood pressure medication to stop taking the medication because it is contradicting their faith or because of what people thought. Never. Never. Never. This is where you have got to remember that your journey is your own and you must see it through until the end.

Now that I have shared some very personal truths about my life and journey-I am determined to NEVER go back to the deep, dark place where I was simply existing in the face of the wind. Now that I have released those who I was holding hostage (my father), I can stay focused. I give you permission to use my experience as a point of reference to show what not forgiving can do to a person. I wasn't perfect then and I am not perfect now. I found out who Vanessa was and I am striving for better every day.

Next time you find yourself depressed I want you to revisit this book, the declarations, and prayers. I want you to rearrange the letters in the word "depression."

The letters rearranged spell out, "I PRESSED ON." Same word different perspective. That's right the fact that you have read and gotten to this point of the book means that you have pressed on. I encourage you to keep pressing on and don't look back no matter what. The diagnosis of depression does not determine or deter your destination. You are still called, chosen, and most importantly love by God.

If you find you need more space to respond to the questions at the Rest Stops you can use the "Journey to Myself" Companion Journal. Your responses in the book and the companion journal can serve as your new beginning and first steps towards total healing. We have finished here with Chapter ten. Your Next is up to you. Healing is your portion. You don't have to stay in the state you're in. Start journaling and making strides towards not only being healed, but becoming whole, and walking in purpose.

"My journey may not have been picture perfect, but it has been perfect for my purpose."
~V.K. Robinson

Thank you for taking a deeper look into parts of my personal journey. It was not easy to share, but I know that someone, somewhere will benefit from my transparency. Look forward to what's next. As a step in a new direction, use the following pages to decide how you will begin again. As you make progress, write down your wins and gains. Use these as points of references when you are having a not so grand day.

Here is one final prayer:

Father, I embrace this journey and I commit everything that has been and will be written to you. You are the captain of my soul and my safe place. Lord you see where I am and the pain I have endured over the years. Lord, I am trusting you to heal me as only you can and make me whole. Lord, I have been disappointed by people, hurt by people, misunderstood by people and offended by people-but today, I choose to forgive them. Lord, I release them from the prison of my heart in order to completely free myself. God, I give you permission, to go where I have not allowed anyone to go before and nurture me with your love and compassion. Father, position me where you want me to be in this life. I surrender wholly to you. I trust you to guide my steps and carry my heart through. I vow not to let go, even in the hard times. I vow to hold on, when everything in me and around me says to quit. God, I vow not to let go and I trust you will not let go of me. Father, use your hands to wipe my tears as I cry the tears that I have been afraid to cry. God, house the screams from the pit of my belly that I was ashamed to release until now. Thank you for hearing my heart utter the things my lips could not articulate. Thank you for being the safe place to sit things that were too heavy for me to carry. God, I thank you and I honor you. I declare no more the same, from this day forward. In Jesus' Name- Amen

Encouraging Scriptures

The scriptures on the following pages are scriptures I used during the darkest times in my life whenever things hit a little different and I find myself in a not so comfortable place. Choose one scripture to meditate on each day as you are journeying and pressing forward.

I would write down the scripture in my journal. Then I would take sticky notes or post-it notes and write the scriptures down. I would post them where I knew I could see them (Beside my bedpost, in my office on the wall in front of my desk, in my bathroom on my side of the mirror, in my car in the sun visor, and on my reading stand). These notes were strategically placed for the times that I could not pray, I could not remember a scripture, I read the posted scripture and prayed the scripture.

One of the very last things I would do is record myself. Yes, record myself reading the scriptures. Of course, I would do this when I was on the up and up as a proactive strategy. Then I would listen to them on those days when I was not feeling my best and I could not really function at normal capacity.

Some may ask why didn't I just listen to the recordings that app could read to me. I'm glad you asked. I needed to hear MYSELF declaring the Word of the Lord over my life. This pushed me. I was the head cheerleader on my bench and I needed to lead with authority. My words and my voice- they matter.

Initially, I was going to simply give you a list of scriptures. After prayer and thought, I decided it was important for me to type the scriptures in this journal.

When you are in a low, dark place, sometimes it is difficult to go through the bible and find the scripture you want. Personally, I would get frustrated when I was in this place and not able to go straight to the bible to find a particular scripture. Just in case you are faced with that situation, the scriptures on the following pages are here to encourage you.

Philippians 4:8
Finally, brethren, whatsoever things are true, whatsoever things are honest, whatsoever things are just, whatsoever things are pure, whatsoever things are lovely, whatsoever things are of good report; if there be any virtue, and if there be any praise, think on these things.

Deuteronomy 31:8
The LORD himself goes before you and will be with you; he will never leave you nor forsake you. Do not be afraid; do not be discouraged.

Psalm 34:17
The righteous cry out, and the LORD hears them; he delivers them from all their troubles.

Psalm 40:1–3
I waited patiently for the LORD; he turned to me and heard my cry. He lifted me out of the slimy pit, out of the mud and mire; he set my feet on a rock and gave me a firm place to stand. He put a new song in my mouth, a hymn of praise to our God. Many will see and fear the LORD and put their trust in him.

Psalm 3:3
But you, LORD, are a shield around me, my glory, the One who lifts my head high.

Psalm 32:10
Many are the woes of the wicked, but the LORD's unfailing love surrounds the one who trusts in him.

Psalm 42:11
Why, my soul, are you downcast? Why so disturbed within me? Put your hope in God, for I will yet praise him, my Savior and my God.

1 Peter 5:6–7
Humble yourselves, therefore, under God's mighty hand, that he may lift you up in due time. Cast all your anxiety on him because he cares for you.

John 16:33
I have told you these things, so that in me you may have peace. In this world, you will have trouble. But take heart! I have overcome the world.

Romans 8:38–39
For I am convinced that neither death nor life, neither angels nor demons, neither the present nor the future, nor any powers, neither height nor depth, nor anything else in all creation, will be able to separate us from the love of God that is in Christ Jesus our Lord.

2 Corinthians 1:3–4
Praise be to the God and Father of our Lord Jesus Christ the Father of compassion and the God of all

comfort, who comforts us in all our troubles, so that we can comfort those in any trouble with the comfort we ourselves receive from God.

1 Peter 4:12–13
Dear friends, do not be surprised at the fiery ordeal that has come on you to test you, as though something strange were happening to you. But rejoice inasmuch as you participate in the sufferings of Christ, so that you may be overjoyed when his glory is revealed.

Psalm 37:23–24
The LORD makes firm the steps of the one who delights in him; though he may stumble, he will not fall, for the LORD upholds him with his hand.

Isaiah 41:10
So, do not fear, for I am with you; do not be dismayed, for I am your God. I will strengthen you and help you; I will uphold you with my righteous right hand.

Jeremiah 29:11
For I know the plans I have for you," declares the LORD, "plans to prosper you and not to harm you, plans to give you hope and a future.

Psalm 23:4
Even though I walk through the darkest valley,[a]

I will fear no evil, for you are with me; your rod and your staff, they comfort me.

Romans 8:37
No, in all these things we are more than conquerors through him who loved us.

John 16:33
I have told you these things, so that in me you may have peace. In this world, you will have trouble. But take heart! I have overcome the world.

Romans 8:28
And we know that all things work together for good to them that love God, to them who are the called according to his purpose.

Matthew 28:20
Teaching them to observe all things whatsoever I have commanded you: and, lo, I am with you always, even unto the end of the world. Amen.

Psalm 27:1
The LORD is my light and my salvation; whom shall I fear? the LORD is the strength of my life; of whom shall I be afraid?

Psalm 9:9
The LORD is a refuge for the oppressed; a stronghold in times of trouble.

John 14: 16-17
And I will ask the Father, and he will give you another advocate to help you and be with you forever— [17] the Spirit of truth. The world cannot accept him, because it neither sees him nor knows him. But you know him, for he lives with you and will be[a] in you.

Matthew 11:28
Come to me, all you who are weary and burdened, and I will give you rest.

Contact Information:

Visit us at: www.vkrobinson.com

Follow me on Social Media

Facebook: VK Robinson Academic Enterprises

Instagram: VKR Enterprises

Made in the USA
Columbia, SC
01 March 2022

56841378R00090